CASTLES ON THE RHINE

"RHEINISCHES LAND" COLLECTION

VOLUME 2

KÖLN

BONN

GODESBERG
R. Godesburg
Rolands-
bogen
R. Landskron
AHR
BURG Rheineck
ANDERNACH
ERZBISCHÖFL·Burg

KÖNIGSWINTER
R. Drachenfels
R. Ockenfels
LINZ · Burg
SCHL· Arenfels
R. Hammerstein

Neuwied
RHEIN

BURGEN AM RHEIN
von Mainz bis Köln

KOBLENZ
MOSEL
SCHL·Stolzenfels
Königstuhl
ZU RHENS
BOPPARD
Kurtrierische
Burg

Ehrenbreitstein
LAHN
BURG Lahneck
Martinsburg
OBER- LAHNSTEIN
Marksburg ÜBER BRAUBACH

R. Sterrenberg
R. Liebenstein ⟩ DIE FEINDLICHEN BRÜDER
BURG Maus
BURG Reichenberg
R. Rheinfels
ST· GOARSHAUSEN
ST· GOAR
BURG Katz
OBERWESEL
Schönburg
BURG Gutenfels
Pfalz BEI KAUB
BURG
Stahleck
BACHARACH
R. Nollig
R· Fürstenberg
LORCH
Heimburg
BURG Sooneck
ASSMANNSHAUSEN
BURG Reichenstein
RÜDESHEIM
Brömserburg
BURG Rheinstein
R. Ehrenfels
Mäuseturm
BINGEN
BURG Klopp
BURG Windeck
HEIDESHEIM

WIESBADEN
ERZBISCHÖFL·
Burg
ELTVILLE

MAINZ

CASTLES ON THE RHINE

39 PHOTOGRAPHS WITH AN INTRODUCTION BY M. J. MEHS

NEW EDITION PREPARED BY

DR. WALTHER OTTENDORF-SIMROCK

PUBLISHED BY WILHELM STOLLFUSS BONN

ILLUSTRATIONS
Aufsberg, Lala; Sonthofen (Allgäu): Seiten 9, 10, 18, 33, 38, 42, 58, 62, 66, 69, 70, 74, 81; Photo Michels, Stromberg (Hunsrück): Seite 29; Retzlaff, Hans, Tann (Rhön): Seite 50; roebild Röhrig, Kurt, Frankfurt a. M.; Seiten 17, 22, 53, 73; Schöning & Co, Lübeck: Seiten 34, 37; Traubenkraut, Ellen, Ettringen: Umschlagbild und Seiten 14, 21, 25, 26, 30, 41, 45, 46, 49, 54, 57, 61, 77; Wildemann, Th., Bonn: Seite 82; Wohlfahrt, G., Bonn-Bad Godesberg (Städt. Verkehrsamt, Bonn-Bad Godesberg): Seite 82; Dr. Wolff & Tritschler, Frankfurt a. M.: Seiten 65, 78.

PICTORIAL MAP
"Castles on the Rhine from Mainz to Cologne" designed by Ludwig Schäfer-Grohe, Fellbach-Stuttgart.

COVER DESIGN : Katz Castle above St. Goarshausen

Best.-Nr. 61 526 4

Blocks for the illustrations: Laudert & Co., Vreden
Printed by: Kleins Druck- und Verlagsanstalt, Lengerich (Westphalia)
Bound by: Buchbender, Bonn · 75ZU7
English translation by: Barry Jones

CONTENTS

The Rhine Castles (continuation)

Introduction

The castles on the Rhine which are such a characteristic feature of the river landscape, were created by the martial spirit of the Middle Ages as purely defensive structures, devoid of all romantic notions. They were built by powerful rulers over sacred and secular territories, on hilltops, and in the lowlands as moated castles to protect their manorial estates and their inhabitants. In many cases the work of breaking the stones and erecting the massive walls and turrets was done by feudal serfs.

Since Roman times the Rhine valley has been a line of communication of vital strategic importance. In the Middle Ages the German emperors used it for their frequent progresses into Italy and wealthy merchants sent their goods along it, up and down-stream. Obviously anyone owning a castle overlooking the valley was in a powerful position, since he was able to survey and regulate the flow of traffic across his particular territory and levy tolls on merchants. This accounts for the large number of castles along the Rhine between Mainz and Bonn, particularly in the narrow strait connecting Bingen and Koblenz. Along this stretch of the river which has a length of only 35 miles, there are more castles than in any other river valley in the world.

BOPPARD AND THE CASTLE OF THE ELECTOR BALDWIN
(Copper plate engraving by Merian, 1646)

HISTORY OF THE RHINE CASTLES BETWEEN MAINZ AND COLOGNE

The historical background of the Rhine castles is of such diversity that it is difficult to give a clear picture.

Ever since the time of Julius Caesar the Rhine has become more and more the real centre of the occident. The possession of a castle on the Rhine was a source of influence and power and enabled its owner to play an important part in the events of the day.

Feudal lords of every rank came to the Rhine headed by kings and emperors in order to profit by the toll fees for which this most important waterway in the old empire offered ample opportunity. Between Mainz and Cologne there were no fewer than thirty different toll barriers. It was, therefore, only natural that every square yard of land was hotly contested and had to be tenaciously defended. This led to the construction of mighty castles which, little by little, were enlarged until they became elaborate edifices the ruins of which even today still fill us with awe. In the numerous feuds heroic resistance was often crushed by a more powerful foe and this explains the fact that in the course of time the castles frequently changed hands.

The feudal overlords

Today the Rhine between Mainz and Cologne flows through three federal states: Rhineland Palatinate, Hesse and North Rhine-Westphalia. But you need only cast a glance at an historical map showing Germany at about the time of the Peace of Westphalia (1648) to see how independent territories and political groups vied with each other for possession of these seats of power on the Rhine in their search for influence and domination of what can truly be described as Germany's river of destiny. No great change took place in this state of affairs until the French Revolution and the Congress of Vienna.

Great Hall in the Marksburg · Text on page 63

BACHARACH AND STAHLECK CASTLE
(Copper plate engraving by Wenzel Hollar around 1638)

In the Middle Ages the Electorate of Mainz was firmly in possession of the upper Rhine because it held the castle of Elfeldt, known today as *Eltville* which, strange to say, had originally been built by the Elector Baldwin of Trier as a defence against Mainz but which he soon ceded to Mainz. But above all the castles of *Klopp* and *Ehrenfels* at the entrance to the Binger Loch, together with the *Mouse Tower* were held by the Mainz Elector. The same applied to *Rheinstein* which about the year 1350 had been in the possession of the Trier Elector for a brief period; and to the castle of *Reichenstein* which was originally a Palatine possession, and the castles of *Sooneck* and *Heimburg.* No traveller along the Rhine could possibly evade this impregnable barrier of toll fortresses many of which were occupied by robber knights.

Further downstream the Elector Palatine staked his claim to the possession first of *Fürstenberg Castle,* formerly belonging to the Cologne Electors which had meanwhile been conquered by Ludwig of Bavaria for a time. Then he

11

14th century carved gravestone of a knight in St. Mary's Cathedral at Oberwesel

sought possession of *Stahleck* which had likewise first belonged to the Cologne Electors and afterwards passed into the hands of the Counts of Katzenelnbogen, various German emperors and finally to the Palatinate in 1214. Further claims by the Elector Palatinate were to the *Pfalz* near Kaub built by Ludwig of Bavaria and to *Gutenfels* built by the Falkensteiners which became Ludwig of Bavaria's favourite residence. The *Schönburg* near Oberwesel, however, property of the Counts of Schönburg, lay within the territory of the Trier electors.

Around St. Goar and St. Goarshausen the Counts of Katzenelnbogen and after their demise about 1500, the Landgrave of Hesse came from the East to dominate the scene, holding *Rheinfels* Castle on the left bank, *Katz* Castle on the right bank and the *Marksburg*. As the counterpart, so to speak, there was the *Maus* Castle near Wellmich held by the Electors of Trier who exercised territorial rights over an extensive area on both sides of the river from the mouth of the Moselle in Koblenz up to Boppard and beyond. The castle in *Boppard*, *Stolzenfels* Castle and *Ehrenbreitstein* are significant witnesses to the power of the Trier electorate as is also the *Kurfürstenburg* in Koblenz which belongs to the Moselle area rather than to the Rhine. In between were the legendary knights' castles of *Sterrenberg* and *Liebenstein* known as the "Enemy Brothers". The former had originally been in Palatine possession, the latter for a time having been held by Trier. And near Rhens there was an enclave belonging to the Cologne electors together with *Lahneck* and *Martinsburg* which were the most northerly toll-posts of the Mainz electorate.

Near Neuwied a new series commences: first with the County of Wied and then in *Andernach* with the Kaiserpfalz, a gift of the Emperor Barbarossa to the Cologne electorate. Downstream from here there are alternate electorates: Trier owned *Hammerstein* and *Arenfels* (which had previously belonged to the Isenburgs); Cologne *Rheineck* (once Palatinate) the castle on the *Drachenfels* and the *Godesburg* together with the Dukedoms of Jülich and Berg extending as far as Cologne which was itself a free imperial city.

Each one of these castles led a life of its own and was subjected to a variety of experiences in the service of its owner. However, what interests us above all is the common destiny that befell them all and we cannot help asking why not a single one of them has been preserved in its original form. When and for what reasons were they destroyed or allowed to fall into decay?

12

Defensive gallery in the Pfalz near Kaub · Text on page 52

The first attack on the Rhine Castles

The 13th century saw the first major attack on a number of castles for which, however, their owners who played an inglorious part, had only themselves to blame. The election of Rudolf of Habsburg had been preceded by a deplorable period of interregnum, a time of internal disintegration during which the brigandage of the robber knights spread. It was in order to fight this plague that the League of Rhenish Cities had been founded in 1254 which cooperated with the spiritual electors in keeping the trade routes and especially the Rhine open to traffic. But this individual initiative on the part of the cities proved to be inadequate; their warriors had, for example, made a vain attack on *Rheinfels* Castle. It was not until King Rudolf raised his powerful arm against them in 1272 that the robbers' dens on the Rhine and elsewhere were relentlessly and mercilessly destroyed. These centres of the robber knights were the castles of *Rheinstein, Reichenstein* and *Sooneck* near Bingen and *Rheineck* near Niederbreisig. The castles were destroyed and summary justice administered to the felons. The robbers' fortress of *Rheinfels* alone proved unassailable.

The Thirty Years' War

The second great onslaught on the Rhine castles came with the religious wars of the 16th and 17th centuries. First there was the turmoil in and around Cologne between 1582 and 1586 which resulted in an imperial reprimand of the Cologne Archbishop Gebhardt Truchsess von Waldburg because he had been converted to the new faith, in consequence of which the castles of *Drachenfels* and *Godesburg* were destroyed. Then the Thirty Years' War, that ill-fated struggle for power between the two confessional factions, brought tribulation to many a Rhine castle. At that time soldiers from all over Europe – imperial troops, soldiers of the Catholic "League" and the Protestant "Union", Frenchmen, Spaniards and Swedes fought for supremacy in the Rhine valley. Each of the belligerents sought to occupy and hold on to the most important strategic positions in this grave ideological struggle. *Eltville,* in those days still known as Elfeldt, *Klopp* Castle, *Ehrenfels* and *Fürstenberg* were held by the Swedes; *Stahleck, Gutenfels* and *Schönburg* were successively attacked and plundered by the Spaniards, the French and the

15

The Archbishop's Castle in Eltville · Text on page 39

Swedes; *Ehrenbreitstein* was captured by the French, *Koblenz* by the Swedes; *Andernach, Hammerstein, Rheineck* and *Drachenfels* were occupied and in some cases bombarded and burnt down by Swedish, imperial and Spanish troops.

The Reunion Wars

The third and for most of the castles, more destructive danger for the region of the Middle Rhine came with the decisions of the Metz Reunion Chamber under the French King Louis XIV. In order to gain sovereignty over German territories, he sent his armies as far as the Rhine to protect his own troops from the rear, conquering and destroying one castle after the other. In 1688 *Klopp, Reichenstein* and *Lahneck* fell; in 1689 *Ehrenfels, Sooneck, Heimburg, Fürstenberg, Stahleck, Schönburg, Maus, Stolzenfels, Andernach, Hammerstein* and *Rheineck*. Of all the beleaguered fortresses Rheinfels was again the only one to withstand even the French attacks.

The period of the French Revolution

The fourth and last blow to be inflicted on the Rhine castles came in the time of the French Revolution. After the canonade of Valmy in 1792 the revolutionary troops forced the German armies to withdraw beyond the Rhine. Those Rhine castles that were still standing or which had been rebuilt and were manned for resistance, were forced to capitulate. The walls were razed to the ground, the stones sold and the occupants expelled. Such was the fate especially of *Gutenfels, Katz, Maus, Rheinfels, Lahneck* and the *Godesburg*.

Since the French Revolution there has no longer been any real history of the Rhine castles. Their former significane was a thing of the past since they were no longer of any use for war purposes and offered no protection against modern artillery and explosives. A few which had not fallen entirely into decay and could be made habitable, became permanent or summer residences.

16

Nollig Castle near Lorch · Text on page 51

The Rhine landscape and the castles

The castles on the Rhine were at one time a part of history. They do not appear as foreign bodies in the landscape but seem to have merged with it and no Rhine traveller of today could imagine this landscape without them. The men who built them were both artists and landscape designers quite unlike the more technically-minded builders of today.

The ancient castles on the Rhine are the work of the creative German spirit and artistic design far beyond the mere functional edifice built for defensive purposes. In their massive ground plans they are hardly less impressive than the romanesque Gothic cathedrals on the Rhine with their spires soaring heavenwards. Where the Rhine landscape, the landscape of "Germany's pulsating artery" – as Görres once described it – called for some distinguishing feature, the builders of these castles provided it. And they did so with such assurance and vitality that they appear to have grown naturally out of the living rock. When one inspects the individual castles more closely – their gates and turrets, their courtyards and chambers, their spiral staircases and apartments, one finds at every turn that each century, each period of artistic style left behind its own typical architecture which, in some cases must even be described as unique in its beauty. Where the interior of the castles have escaped destruction, there are castle chapels, art collections, libraries, archives and arsenals containing all kinds of weapons to prove that the feudal lords of these castles led lives of culture, that they were truly representative of the centuries in which they lived, being both patriots and protectors of the landscape, creators and patrons of art and science who made their castles real centres of life and culture.

The castle as a structure of defence and defiance

With what idea in mind were these castles built? In accordance with what laws were they planned and further developed? The following outline is intended to answer these questions since it contains all the components of a castle fortress.

Originally castles were intended to be fortified residences for feudal lords who sought to protect themselves against attack. The earliest form of castle, therefore, was a building with very thick walls the ground floor of which, apart

19

Klopp Castle above Bingen · Text on page 43

from having a gate that could be securely barred from the inside, revealed scarcely any other opening. The gate was particularly well protected on the outside by a deep moat which could only be crossed by a drawbridge. In the course of time additions were made to this early kind of fortress according to the space available. In most cases the first addition was a courtyard surrounded, of course, by a high wall surmounted by battlements and parapets, sometimes with its own gatehouse for the operation of the drawbridge. Subsequently further outbuildings were added round the courtyard which were always protected against any potential attacker by strong walls. These outbuildings gradually assumed the functions originally concentrated in the central building.

The central building or *palas* (marked in the sketch as 1) contained the residential quarters of the lord or knight and included the kitchen, living rooms, ladies' retiring rooms, a banqueting hall, the baronial hall, sleeping quarters and other accommodation such as a library and a room for hunting trophies.

At a point giving the most favourable view of the surrounding countryside was the *keep* (2), a tall tower with pinnacles and turrets towering above the surrounding buildings. This was the look-out from which all movements in the vicinity of the castle as well as beyond could be observed. During an assault on the castle it was the central command post from which the defence of the castle was directed. At times the underground vaults were used as dungeons unless some other part of the subterranean quarters were used for this purpose.

Attached to the residential quarters or forming part of them was the *Castle Chapel* (3), often a building of great architectural beauty. The castle chaplains were, in many cases, descended from the same noble family as their overlords.

Where space permitted and the need existed there were the necessary *service quarters* (4) such as servants' rooms, toll house, stables, barn, granary, tithe barn, workshop, smithy, arsenal, carpenter's shop, well-house, brewery, poultry house, peacock house – some of them located over the mighty vaulted cellars which contained a plentiful supply of mature wines stored in massive casks.

20

The Mäuseturm in the Binger Loch and the ruins of Ehrenfels · *Text on page 43*

DIAGRAMMATIC LAY-OUT OF A CASTLE
1 living quarters (palas), 2 Keep, 3 Chapel, 4 Service or Domestic buildings, 5 Outworks,
6 Drawbridges, 7 Turrets, 8 Defensive gallery

All that has been described so far formed part of the *Main Castle,* in front of which were the *outer works* (5) of the castle. It is astonishing how the builders managed to utilize every fissure, protrusion and slope in the solid rock for the purpose of the castle. The *outer works* were a kind of outer court for the main fortification, secured on all sides by *drawbridges* (6) and no less protected than the Main Castle by buttresses and battlements, *turrets* (7), parapets, shooting slits and machicolations, with *ramparts* (8) garrets and pinnacles. The outer works also had their own gatehouse which was specially protected by a portcullis.

The construction and completion of a castle continued, in most cases, over a period of centuries; because again and again new means of improving its defences were discovered. Every castle is thus a variation of the same theme, a highly peculiar alternation between walls, moats and battlements, between courtyards, inner and outer baileys, ramparts and outer bastions, prison yards and dungeons, residential quarters and service buildings, outer, middle and inner gates.

23

The ruins of Ehrenfels Castle near Rüdesheim · Text on page 43

Even though all these features do not apply to every castle on the Rhine, the above general description is, on the whole, accurate.

The castles in the poetry of the 18th and 19th centuries

Perched on the mountain peaks – or, as is more often the case with the Rhine castles – clinging to their slopes, the castles on the Rhine have a particular fascination for people of our own age, even though they have faded into the background of history. This is also the way travellers felt as they sailed up and down the Rhine at the beginning of last century: Dutchmen and Englishmen, Frenchmen and Germans. And their experience of the great river was expressed in the words of the poets, one of the greatest of them being *Goethe* in his younger years, already known for his "Götz" and "Werther" who, at the sight of one of the Rhine castles was inspired to write his poem "Hoch auf dem alten Turm". In July 1774 he was travelling down the River Lahn together with Lavater and Basedow and when the Rhine

DRACHENFELS CASTLE
(Copper plate engraving by Merian, around 1640)

Rheinstein Castle above Trechtingshausen · Text on page 44

valley opened up before him and he set eyes for the first time on Lahneck Castle, he wrote: "Hoch auf dem alten Turme".

These verses are a milestone in the history of German poetry. The emergence of the Rhine in German literature, the awareness of the grandeur of Germany's past and all that later played such a great and lasting role in the romantic beauties and associations of the Rhine and its castles, springs from Goethe's first sight of Lahneck Castle.

Hölderlin's first impression of the Rhine which he recorded in his travel journal in 1788, Count *Friedrich Leopold von Stolberg's* description of his journey from Bonn to Mainz (1791/92) and also the magnificent account given by *Heinrich von Kleist* of his Rhine trip in 1801, mark the beginning of that flood of 19th century travel reports in which so much space is devoted to the Rhine and its castles. Typical of many writers of that time was the work of *Johanna Schopenhauer*, the philosopher's mother, who in her "Excursion to the Rhine" (1816) recorded her impressions of the castles as follows: "Imagine, in addition to the sublime spendour of natural beauty, the many picturesque ruins of old castles gazing sternly down from the rocky eminences into the valley. During the whole length of our journey we were within sight of at least one such ruin, often of more than one, and each has its distinctive peculiarities of architecture and situation. I felt that I was turning over the leaves of some old collection of landscape prints, so rapidly does one interesting scene follow on the heels of the last. In truth one has not eyes to see everything. Behind Assmannshausen the ruins of Sooneck Castle sit enthroned on a high rock; and just beyond this the river widens out until it almost resembles a lake, on which to my astonishment I thought I beheld a great warship with spreading sails; but it was the Pfalz, a castle built in the middle of the Rhine. Opposite are the dark walls of the old town of Kaub, and high above these again the proud ruins of Gutenfels Castle. Behind the pleasant little town of St. Goar rise the walls of Rheinfels which was destroyed in the Revolutionary Wars. More ruins overlook St. Goarshausen, and at an angle from this, in the distance, the remains of two further castles are visible. I cannot describe to you the beauty and sublimity of this landscape which now at sunset lay pink and glimmering before us. I could not tear myself away from it until all had faded in the last embers of the dying sun."

27

Heimburg Castle in Niederheimbach · Text on page 48

Symbols of Rhine romanticism

Josef von Eichendorff while still a student at Heidelberg, paid homage to the castles of the Middle Rhine in his poem "Auf einer Burg", and *Clemens* and *Bettina Brentano,* that brother and sister who had so much spiritually in common, held romantic dialogues with the ruins of the Rhine castles. The castles became the symbols of Rhine romanticism. Poets of the Wars of Liberation like *Max von Schenckendorf, Ernst Moritz Arndt* and others glorified them in verse. Scholars like *Nikolaus Vogt* and *Karl Simrock,* after years of painstaking research as collectors and compilers, published their Rhine sagas which, in the course of the centuries had become as much an integral part of the castles as the ivy clinging to their grey walls.

An international heritage

The poets of other nations too have paid tribute to the romanticism of the Rhine castles. In the first chapter of her book "De l'Allemagne", *Madame de Staël* who sees the Rhineland landscape with the eyes of a *Friedrich Schlegel,* speaks of the "débris des châteaux forts", and *Victor Hugo,* leading figure in French romanticism, colourfully portrays the romantic world of ruined castles in his "Le Rhin" which appeared in Paris in 1841. But before this, in 1816, *Byron,* in the third canto of his "Childe Harold's Pilgrimage", had written: "The castled crag of Drachenfels/Frowns o'er the wide and winding Rhine".

The Rhine and its castles also form the romantic background to *Longfellow's* "The Golden Legend" (1843). And so the castles on the Rhine had become part of the cultural heritage of almost the entire civilized world.

Castle-lovers to the rescue

When the Rolandsbogen, a ruined arch above Rolandseck, collapsed on New Year's Eve, 1840, *Ferdinand Freiligrath,* who was then living in Unkel, published a passionate appeal for the reconstruction of the ruin. This appeal resulted in numerous castle-lovers making generous contributions which

28

Reichenstein Castle near Trechtingshausen · Text on page 47

THE FORTIFICATION OF EHRENBREITSTEIN
AT THE TIME OF THE THIRTY YEARS' WAR
(Copper plate engraving by Merian 1646)

enabled the arch to be rebuilt by the Cologne Cathedral architect, *E. F. Zwirner.*

The Biedermeier style which followed the period of romanticism from about 1830 onwards and which Günter Weydt described as "a style of conservation and collecting", gave a powerful stimulus to all efforts aimed at that time at preventing the increasing decay of the castles and at ensuring their preservation for posterity. There were more or less successful attempts partially or entirely to rebuild the ruins and to fit them out as summer residences for the nobility. Their new owners then sought to fill the castles with new life, a life "characterized by the spirit of the Middle Ages". They filled the rooms with old furniture from past centuries or with artistic reproductions in the Biedermeier style. By introducing collections of paintings and coats of arms, an assortments of glassware and pewter, suits of armour, weapons, documents and books the castles acquired the character of a museum.

The Prussian royal family took a particular interest in this revival of the Rhine castles: King Friedrich Wilhelm IV commissioned the architect Friedrich Karl *Schinkel* to rebuild the ruins of *Stolzenfels* Castle, which had been presented to him by the city of Koblenz, in a neo-Gothic style with a pro-

31

Sooneck Castle below Trechtingshausen · Text on page 47

liferation of towers and turrets. Crown-Prince Friedrich Wilhelm and Prince Friedrich of Prussia who were now the owners of the castles of *Sooneck* and *Rheinstein,* had them rebuilt in the same style. They were then furnished in such a way as to make them equally acceptable as residences or as museums. The same was done for *Rheineck* Castle near Niederbreisig. Its artistic owner Moritz August von Bethmann-Hollweg, engaged Joseph Karl *Lassaulx* to redesign the castle in 1832.

Fürstenberg Castle above Rheindiebach · Text on page 48

Historicism and the care of ancient monuments

Although the love of ancient castles that prevailed in the Romanticist period and the fashion of collecting and conservation of the Biedermeier years never entirely disappeared but have continued to the present day, the historicism of the latter half of the 19th century gave greater scope to a scientific approach to the study of history. At the end of the 19th and the beginning of the 20th century views changed once again. The old castles became a subject of interest in the field of the care of ancient monuments, that is to say they "incorporated an historical and cultural value which was to be conserved and cultivated" *(Magnus Backes)*. At this point tribute must be paid to the work of an association which had set itself the task of preserving the castles and of conducting scientific research into all questions connected with medieval fortifications. This was the *Association for the Preservation of German Castles* which was founded in 1899. For many years the driving force in this association was the architect *Bodo Ebhardt* who, himself, conducted much research into German castles. As custodian of the *Marksburg* which Kaiser Wilhelm II presented to the association, he distinguished himself by his reconstruction of that castle in the historic medieval style and also by his work in restoring and protecting numerous other German castles. Bodo Ebhardt was also responsible for the creation of the largest library in Europe consisting of books devoted to medieval castles. Today the *Deutsche Burgenvereinigung zum Schutze historischer Wehrbauten, Schlösser und Wohnbauten e. V.* at Marksburg near Brauchbach, is continuing the work of the original association in an exemplary manner. It is the main information centre for all questions connected with castle building and restoration work. It is planned to set up a German Castles Research Institute based on the library mentioned above and including archives covering all German fortified buildings and castles, a card index system for German castles and the picture archives at present being compiled.

View of Bacharach from Stahleck Castle · Text on page 51

The Present

As a result of two world wars and the continued influence of materialism, the general attitude to these ancient castles has again undergone a change. The more we turn our backs on romanticism and historicism, the more do practical considerations take priority. Insofar as the castles are thought about at all, they are looked upon from the point of view of the use to which they can be put and the advisability of investing money in them. Most of them are now open to visitors and offer facilities for refreshment. Some of them like *Rheinstein, Sooneck, Marksburg* and *Stolzenfels,* are museums; others like *Stahleck, Schönburg Katz Castle* and *Gutenfels,* are youth hostels. While their parents and grandparents were content with no more than a fleeting glance at the castles on the Rhine, the young people of today live in them and with them, gaining a new understanding of history and a respect for the achievements of former generations. For instance, when members of the youth groups belonging to the European Union meet at *Gutenfels* Castle, their discussions are inspired by a living historical consciousness which is more than a mere musty veneration. Many of them realize that the Rhine castles are not merely dead relics of a time long since past but that they have become a living part of the process of time, a time in which people see a new and meaningful purpose for these grey guardians of this great European river.

Stahleck Castle above Bacharach · Text on page 51

THE RHINE CASTLES

The Archbishop's Castle in Eltville

Picture on page 14

The Episcopal Castle on the banks of the Rhine at Eltville with its defiant-looking keep is a landmark that is visible far and wide. It was founded by the factious Archbishop Balduin of Trier in the struggle with Mainz about the year 1330. In the years that followed Eltville or "Alta Villa" which on illustrations around the year 1800 was still named Elfeldt, became the residence of the Archbishops of Mainz. One of them, Berthold von Henneberg, enlarged the castle in 1487. In 1636 it was burnt down by the Swedes. Apart from the mighty keep flanked by rectangular turrets, part of the dungeons and the castle moats were left intact. It was across these moats of the former moated castle that a bridge led from the town into the castle courtyard surrounded by three wings of the building. The keep which was intended chiefly to provide protection against attack by land, formed the south-east cornerstone of the fortifications, whilst the palas or living quarters was located on the less vulnerable side overlooking the Rhine.

In the "Grafensaal" (Hall of the Counts) of this castle, Gutenberg, the inventor of printing, received the only tribute paid to him during his lifetime when he was appointed a court nobleman by the Mainz Elector Adolf II of Nassau. This honour provided the impoverished inventor with security for his old age.

Today, in recognition of the services of Johannes Gutenberg as the inventor of book printing, a memorial centre and an old printer's workshop are to be found in the castle tower. The town authorities who acquired the castle from the former state of Prussia in 1936, today use the representative rooms of the East wing for cultural purposes, receptions and council meetings.

Owned by the Municipality of Eltville. Partly inhabited; Gutenberg Memorial. – Reached by car from the Rhine embankment; car park – from there, three minutes walk. – Open to the public throughout the year every day except Mondays. Apply to castle warden.

Gutenfels Castle above Kaub · Text on page 52

Windeck Castle in Heidesheim

This little moated castle situated at the northern end of Heidesheim, in addition to a moat formed by a diversion of the Sülzbach and the remains of the interior defensive wall, also possessed a circular wall which, today, has entirely disappeared. The best preserved part of the castle is its massive tower which is probably the oldest residential tower in Hesse, having been built by Herdegen von Winternheim about the year 1200. All that is left of the wooden parapet walk which used to circumvent the tower are a few old beams. The building housing the living quarters and located round three sides of the tower, dates from the end of the 16th century.

When the last of the Winternheim family died towards the end of the 14th century, the property passed into the possession of the Mainz Electorate which then assigned the castle to its district administrator as his official residence.

From 1609 onwards at the latest, it was an hereditary castle and had various owners, one of them being Jan van Werth, famous cavalry general of the Thirty Years' War. When the castle and its contents were auctioned by the French, Windeck Castle, formerly also known as Wintereck, passed into private ownership.

Owned by Käthe Wehner. Inhabited. – Not open to the public.

The Three Castles in Rüdesheim

The castles of the Knights of Rüdesheim today still dominate the scene in this old wine town.

The Lower Castle of *Brömserburg* was probably built as a moated castle about the year 1000 and is today still one of the most notable examples of Romanesque castle architecture. Grouped around the mighty keep, it was used until well into the 13th century by the archbishops of Mainz who, in the years that followed, handed it over to the Brömser family of Rüdesheim. Today the Brömserburg houses the *Rheingau Museum*.

Owned by the town of Rüdesheim. Rheingau Museum and Wine Museum. – Reached by car; Car park. – Open daily.

Gutenfels Castle and the Pfalz near Kaub · Text on page 52

The Upper Castle of *Boosenburg* is also a former moated castle, occupied since the 13th century by the Füchse family of Rüdesheim and between 1474 and 1830 by the Barons Boos von Waldeck. Frequent alterations were made to the castle and only the early Romanesque tower which is 38 metres high is still standing.

Owner: Dr. Carl Jung, Vineyard and Wine Distillery. – Reached by car from the Rhine road, Niederstrasse. Car park in courtyard.

The *Marktburg* situated close to the market place is one of the oldest castles in the Rheingau. It belonged to the "Herren vom Markte" (Lords of the Market), a family which died out in the 16th century. All that remains of the castle is a Romanesque tower some 25 metres high.

Owned by Vineyard Johann Schön Erben. Inhabited. – Reached by car. – On view subject to owner's consent.

Klopp Castle above Bingen

Picture on page 18

Klopp Castle, one of the rare hilltop castles on the Rhine, was built on the foundations of a Roman fortress (Roman well). In 1420 the castle passed into the possession of the Mainz Cathedral Chapter on whose orders it was demolished in 1713. In 1789, in the course of the Palatinate War of Succession, it was rebuilt. Since 1897 it has been the office of the municipal administration.

The tower of Klopp Castle houses the local history museum containing some valuable collections. Here the instruments of a Roman doctor of the 2nd century after Christ are particularly worth seeing.

Owned by the town of Bingen. Houses the local municipal administration. Local history museum (open daily from April 15 to October 15). Restaurant (with Rhinegold Hall). – Reached by car. – Car park in the castle courtyard. – Open to the public daily except Mondays.

Ehrenfels Castle near Rüdesheim

Pictures on pages 21, 22

The Mainz electoral castle dating from the first half of the 13th century, together with Klopp Castle on the opposite side and the Mouse Tower formed a solid defence of the electorate to the North. Situated half-way up the

43

The Pfalz near Kaub · Text on page 52

rock-side at the entrance to the Binger Loch, it was a vital strategic point in the Middle Ages located as it was, fairly low overlooking the river. At the same time the Ehrenfels toll was an important source of revenue for the Mainz archbishops who enlarged and improved it in accordance with its importance, making it one of the most magnificent castles on the Rhine. In times of war the treasures of Mainz Cathedral were stored there. The castle was destroyed in 1689 but with its mighty face wall facing the hill on which it stands and flanked by two circular corner towers, the ruins present a most picturesque scene. Those prepared to make the effort to climb the steep paths leading through the vineyards will be well rewarded by the beautiful view of the Rhine valley which Karl Simrock described as "one of the most glorious, even perhaps the most magnificent to be seen anywhere in the Rhine valley".

Owned by the Land of Hesse. Administration of state vineyards in Eltville. – Reached on foot in 30 minutes from Rüdesheim, from Rhine road (B 42) level crossing 15 minutes. – Closed to the public owing to the danger of collapse.

Rheinstein Castle

Picture on page 25

Situated only eighty metres above the river and built on a projecting rock, Rheinstein Castle, formerly known as Voitsburg or Feitsburg, was first mentioned in ancient documents in 1279. In fact it had been established by the Archbishops of Mainz as a toll station even before Ehrenfels. In the year 1348 it came into the possession of the Trier Elector Kuno von Falkenstein, the powerful archbishop who, in his time, ruled over all three archbishoprics on the Rhine. In 1825 the ruins of the castle were acquired by the art-loving Prince Friedrich of Prussia who had them restored in the neo-Gothic style by the architect Wilhelm Kühn on the basis of plans by Joseph Carl von *Lassaulx*. The castle has been described by Paul Clemen as "this notable early monument of romantic castle architecture on the Rhine". In addition to its valuable interior furnishings dating from the beginning of the 19th century, Rheinstein Castle also contains valuable *collections of armour and art treasures* including especially, handicrafts of the 16th and 17th centuries.

Owned by Duchess Barbara zu Mecklenburg, née Princess of Prussia. Museum, Restaurant. – Reached by car from Koblenz and Bingen (B 9); car park below the castle. – 5 minutes walk from car park. – Conducted tours at all times in various languages.

Oberwesel with St. Martin's Church, St. Mary's Cathedral and Schönburg Castle
Text on page 55

Reichenstein Castle

Picture on page 29

Above St. Clement's Chapel (12th century) romantically situated on the banks of the river, and at the end of the Morgenbach Valley, rises Reichenstein Castle, one of the oldest castles on the Rhine. First mentioned in 1213 as the possession of Kornelimünster Abbey which had it administered by a castellan, this castle developed into a den of robber knights and, in 1253, it was destroyed for the first time by the League of Rhenish Cities. Then in 1282 it was Rudolf von Habsburg who had it razed to the ground – the castle having in the meantime passed into the possession of the Mainz electorate and having been rebuilt. After again being restored, the castle was, for a long time, a bone of contention between the electorates of Mainz and the Palatinate. The imposing outer wall facing the hillside probably dates from the 14th century. In 1689 it was again destroyed, this time by the French. But it was rebuilt in 1900 by the father of the present owner and today houses a very important *collection of antlers and weapons*.

Owned by Baron Kirsch-Puricelli. Valuable collections. Castle Hotel with restaurant – Reached by car from Trechtingshausen via the B 9; car park in the castle courtyard. – 5 minutes walk from the B 9. – Conducted tours daily every 20 minutes (except November and December). Large parties by prior appointment. Telephone: Bingen 0 67 21/61 17 or 61 01.

Sooneck Castle

Picture on page 30

Sooneck is the frontier fortress on the edge of the Soon Forest, the fringe of which extends almost down to the Rhine valley. It is one of the oldest castles on the Rhine. The original building dates back to the time of Archbishop Willegis of Mainz around the year 1000. In the 13th century it was already notorious as a den of robber knights. It is one of the castles that were besieged and destroyed by King Rudolf von Habsburg in order to bring peace to the area. In about 1350 it was entirely rebuilt. In 1689 the castle was in ruins, and it was acquired by Crown Prince Friedrich Wilhelm of Prussia in 1834 from the town of Niederheimbach. He had it rebuilt in the neo-Gothic style as had been the case with the castles of Rheinstein and Stolzenfels. A leading art historian named Paul Clemen, deplored the fact that too many battlements and arched mouldings had been added to the large

47

Schönburg Castle above Oberwesel · Text on page 55

rectangular structure with its corner turrets. Inside the tower there is a *beautiful collection of old Rhine views.* The castle is impressively situated, perched high on a crest of the hill over the "Soonecker Grund".

Owned by the Land Rhineland-Palatinate. Refreshments. Museum. – Reached by car from Niederheimbach (B 9). Car park. – 30 minutes walk from the Rhine road. – Open to the public daily from 9 a. m. to 6 p. m.

Hohneck Castle (also known as Heimburg)

Picture on page 26

Above the long row of houses of Niederheimbach, the ivy-covered Hohneck Castle is lower down the hillside and thus closer to the river than any of the Rhine castles. The 13th century castle with its face wall towards the hillside and its 25 metre high keep, forms the northern defensive corner-post of the Mainz electorate against the electorate of the Palatinate. After being in ruins since the 17th century, it was rebuilt in the second half of the 19th century.

Owned by Paulheinz Kann. – Not open to the public.

Fürstenberg Castle

Picture on page 33

The ruins of this castle situated on a rocky spur above the village of Rheindiebach, formerly served as a toll castle for the Palatine Electorate. The tower of the castle especially, attracted the attention of Victor Hugo who wrote of it as follows: "How strange is its extraordinary height and its unusual lay-out. It stands there with its high battlements but with no surrounding wall, no openings or windows and with hardly any arrow slits, its circumference and thickness increasing from the top downwards ..."

In 1321 Ludwig of Bavaria besieged and conquered the castle which was first mentioned in 1243. Even he wished for nothing else here on the Rhine but to levy tolls from passing ships in order to fill his coffers. In 1632 Fürstenberg Castle was captured by the Swedes during the Thirty Years' War and in 1689, the fortress was destroyed by French troops and it has been in ruins ever since. Our photograph gives one a good idea of the old fortress and of the defensive value of the castle. Immediately behind the deep ditch on the side facing the hill, there used to be a gatehouse, the former location

48

Katz Castle above St. Goarshausen · Text on page 56

of which is today just a heap of rubble. All that is left of its former so mighty surrounding wall is just an ivy-covered ruin. Of the palas or living quarters too, there is nothing to be seen but rubble overgrown with shrubbery. The tower alone which tapers to a height of 25 metres seems to have been built for eternity.

Owned by Vineyard Wasum, Bacharach. – Not open to the public.

Nollig Castle
Picture on page 17

Situated on an elevation above Lorch at the end of the Wisper Valley, this castle once formed part of the town fortifications. First mentioned around 1100. A tower furnished as a residence and two corner turrets on the side facing the hill have been rebuilt by the owner.

Owned by Fritz Wild. – Not open to the public.

Stahleck Castle
Pictures on pages 34, 37

The copper plate engraving by Wenzel Hollar shows Stahleck prior to its destruction by the Swedes in 1632. The artist sought to give an objective portrayal of the castle together with the defensive system of the town of Bacharach. One can clearly recognize the circular keep, two smaller towers and the stately palas or living quarters. The attacking front of the castle was that facing the hill. The side facing the Rhine seems invulnerable, protected as it is by the steeply sloping hillside and the town walls. The wall with its fortified turrets leading down into the valley – its remains are still clearly visible – unites town and castle in one powerful fortress.

Stahleck which is one of the most famous Rhine castles of the Middle Ages, was first mentioned in the year 1135. Originally it was the most southerly possession of the archbishops of Cologne; in 1190 the Emperor Barbarossa transferred ownership to his brother Konrad. When the latter's daughter Agnes secretly married her childhood friend Heinrich the Guelph, son of Heinrich the Lion, against the will of her father, the marriage taking place at Stahleck Castle, it brought to an end the bitter feud between the Staufers and the Guelphs. On the death of Agnes and of her only son who was child-

51

Maus Castle above Wellmich · Text on page 60

less, Emperor Friedrich II transferred the expired tenure to the Wittelsbacher Ludwig of Bavaria in 1214. Hence this powerful family then possessed with Stahleck and Pfalz Castles, two important bases on the Rhine.

The castle destroyed in 1689 was rebuilt as a superb reproduction of the original by the Rhenish Association for the Care of Ancient Monuments who placed it at the disposal of the German Youth Hostel Association for use as a castle hostel for young people.

Owned by the German Youth Hostel Association, Land of Rhineland-Palatinate. Youth Hostel. – Reached by car from Bacharach; car park. – 20 minutes walk from Bacharach. – Open to visitors only by appointment.

The Pfalz near Kaub

Pictures on pages 13, 41, 42

"A ship of stone eternally floating on the Rhine, eternally at anchor in full view of the Count Palatine's town" (Victor Hugo), is the Pfalz formerly known as the Pfalzgrafenstein (Count Palatine's Rock) – one of the most curious fortified structures in the world. The only other castle to which it can be compared is, perhaps, Chillon Castle in Lake Geneva.

It was built as an island fortress prior to 1327, the year in which it is first mentioned, by King Ludwig the Bavarian for the purpose of levying tolls on the Rhine. From the spacious courtyard surrounded by pillared arcades and passages made of wood, the stumpy, pentagonal shaped tower rises. In the course of the centuries the shape of the roof of this tower has been changed on various occasions. The observation turrets protruding at the corners were constructed in their present form in the 17th century. The southern corner of this "ship of stone" housed the living quarters and there used to be an entry hatch there together with a ladder.

Owned by the Land of Rhineland-Palatinate. – Reached by ferry from Kaub. – Open daily from 10 a. m. to noon and from 2 p. m. to 5 p. m.; Apply to Gustav von Eicken, Kaub, Bahnstrasse 26a.

Gutenfels Castle

Pictures on pages 38, 41

Built in the first half of the 13th century, this castle which was first mentioned in ancient documents in 1257, was in the possession of the Falkenstein

The ruins of Rheinfels above St. Goar · Text on page 59

family from which Archbishop Kuno von Falkenstein of Trier came. But only 20 years later the castle together with the town of Kaub lying at its feet, came into the possession of the Palatine Elector. It received the name Gutenfels in 1504 after the Landgrave Wilhelm of Hesse had beleaguered it in vain.

The stately palas or living quarters has a large hall in each of its three storeys and the window arches of these halls are partly circular, partly pointed and in some cases even clover-leaf shape. The imposing 35 metre high tower is in a splendid state of preservation. "With its variety of late Romanesque shapes, Gutenfels Castle gives one an excellent idea of the structure and lay-out of a castle on the Rhine" (Paul Clemen). The fact that this is so is due to the Hessian archivist Habel, himself a castle lover, who acquired Gutenfels in 1833 intending to save this architectural monument. In 1886 the Cologne Cathedral architect Walther refurnished the castle.

Owned by Willi Maurer, Boppard. Castle hotel open at weekends. (Enquiries should be addressed to Verwaltung Burg Gutenfels, 5425 Kaub). – Reached by car from Kaub; car park. – 15 minutes walk. – Not open to the public.

Schönburg Castle above Oberwesel

Pictures on pages 45, 46

The town of Oberwesel with its many spires and towers, extolled by Freiligrath as "the most beautiful refuge on the Rhine of the Romantic period", is dominated from the South by Schönburg Castle, the majestic grandeur of which makes it one of the mightiest castle fortifications on the Rhine. On the landward side is the "Hohe Mantel", the huge angular wall which is indeed an awe-inspiring structure designed to protect the two keeps and the living quarters. At a very early date the castle was recorded as an imperial tenure in the possession of the Lords of Schönenberg or Schomberg who provided the burgraves and overseers of Oberwesel. In the 14th century when it was the subject of dispute between the Reich, Trier and the Palatinate, it was enlarged by two branches of the family which also built their own castle houses known as "parcenary houses". The castle which, in 1689 together with the town, was gutted by fire and destroyed, was acquired in the 1880s by the German-American Rhinelander who, at very considerable expense, restored it. After the last war the part facing the Rhine was modernized but

55

Reichenberg Castle near St. Goarshausen · Text on page 56

its ancient character was preserved and it was converted into an International Kolping Youth Hostel.

Owned by the town of Oberwesel. Castle hotel and restaurant. – Reached by car from Oberwesel station. Car park. – 15 minutes walk from the station along two winding paths leading off from Fahrstrasse.

Katz Castle

Picture on page 49

This mighty castle is set like a crown on the hill overlooking St. Goarshausen. Its real name is "Neu-Katzenelnbogen". It was built by Johann III. in the year 1393 for the protection of the County of Katzenelnbogen. In 1479, the "Katz" as the castle was known for short, passed into the possession of the Landgraves of Hesse-Kassel. It was not until 1804 that it was destroyed by the French. In 1896/98 it was rebuilt by Bodo Ebhardt and today houses the Hofmann Institute, a natural science grammar and boarding school. The massive circular keep protecting the three-storey palas or living quarters is particularly imposing. The access path leads under the palas into the narrow castle courtyard. The view especially southwards to the Loreley is rightly regarded as one of the most famous on the Rhine.

Owned by the German Federal Republic. Holiday home of the Federal Social Welfare Organization. Not open to the public.

Reichenberg Castle

Picture on page 54

Reichenberg Castle near St. Goarshausen, situated a few kilometres inland in the Hasenbachtal, is considered by art historians to be the most outstanding castle fortress in the Rhineland. The building was started by Count Wilhelm I. of Katzenelnbogen in the year 1320 to take the place of an older castle that had formerly stood there. But the plan was on such a grandiose scale that it was never completed. The wide protective wall extended between two slender circular towers. A notable feature of the castle is the three-storey hall building supported by pillars. As the floors have disappeared "three pillars stand one above the other, seeming to juggle with the high cross vault, a truly fantastic sight" (Richard Klapheck). Unfortunately the northern tower and parts of the wall collapsed in 1971.

Owned by Friedrich Holz. Inhabited. – Inspection impossible owing to danger of collapse.

The "Enemy Brothers" Sterrenberg and Liebenstein · Text on page 60

Rheinfels Castle

Picture on page 53

In the year 1245 Count Diether V. von Katzenelnbogen had the castle built for the protection of the St. Goar toll and within a short time it was developed into one of the most powerful castle fortresses in the central Rhine area. Only ten years after the commencement of the building work, Rheinfels Castle was successfully defended for a whole year in 1255 against a powerful army of the Rhenish League of Towns.

In the course of the following century the original toll castle became the increasingly important centre of administration of the Counts of Katzenelnbogen who, by their astute financial and marriage policy, became one of the leading families in the central Rhine area.

The construction of the Neukatzenelnbogen Castle (today known briefly as *Katz* Castle) on the other side of the Rhine in the 14th century, the importance of Rheinfels Castle was further increased since the counts were now able to exercise complete and effective control of the Rhine valley.

When in 1479 the family of the Counts of Katzenelnbogen died out when at the height of their territorial power, Rheinfels Castle passed into the possession of the Landgraviate of Hesse. – Under the Hessian Landgraves *Rheinfels* was converted into a magnificent Renaissance castle and, together with its exterior fortifications, was enlarged to make it one of the most formidable fortresses in Germany. In 1692 *Rheinfels*, as the only fortress on the left bank of the Rhine, was successfully defended against the troops of Louis XIV. But when, in 1794, the fortress was surrendered without a fight to the French Revolutionary Army, the end of this proud castle had really come. In 1796/97 the castle together with its outer fortifications was demolished.

The visitor who inspects Rheinfels Castle today will be surprised at the vast extent of the ruins and at the maze of walled passages and underground adits which can still be walked along today. – But a really all-round impression of the military and cultural importance of the castle can only be obtained by studying the ancient plans and historical views of this once proud fortress, to be found in the former castle chapel where, today, the local history collection is housed.

Owned by the town of St. Goar. Partly inhabited. Local history museum. Restaurant and hotel. – Reached by car from St. Goar and from Hunsrück. – Car park. – 15 minutes walk from St. Goar. 45 minutes walk from Gründelbachtal (Hansenweg). – Open daily during the summer season.

Liebenstein Castle above Kamp-Bornhofen · Text on page 60

Maus Castle

Picture on page 50

Where there is a cat there must also be a mouse – that is what the Counts of Katzenelnbogen are reported to have said so scornfully of the new Trier electoral castle which, in the course of thirty years of building work from 1353 onwards had slowly taken shape above the town of Wellmich. The ulterior motive here, of course, was that the mouse would soon be caught by the cat and devoured. Its real name was originally Peterseck and then Thurnberg. The castle was ultimately completed by the great Trier Archbishop Kuno von Falkenstein who died here in 1388. Maus Castle is, architecturally, one of the most beautiful to be found along the Rhine. The almost square-shaped outline encloses a circular keep protruding from the main wall, a fours-torey residential tower and the stately palas along the entire South side. Walled passages and the projecting corner turrets on all sides testify to the defensive nature of the castle and also to the fine intellectual spirit of that time. Between 1900 and 1906 the castle was carefully restored with laudable attention to historical detail.

Owned by M. S. M. Grundstücksges. m. b. H., Berlin. – Not open to the public.

The "Enemy Brothers" Sterrenberg and Liebenstein

Pictures on pages 57, 58

The two castle ruins of Sterrenberg and Liebenstein which are situated on rocky crags above the ancient pilgrim town of Bornhofen are popularly known as the "enemy brothers".

Sterrenberg is the older of the two and as early as the 12th century it was in the possession of the Palatine family, the Lords of Bolanden as an imperial castle. Later it was owned by the Counts of Sponheim. Archbishop Balduin incorporated it in the Trier electorate. The square keep is still standing and the two protective walls can be clearly recognized. These walls were designed to screen Sterrenberg off on the side facing the hill and against the neighbouring castle.

Owned by the Land Rhineland-Palatinate. Inhabited. Castle restaurant. – Reached by car from Kamp-Bornhofen (B 42) via Burgenstrasse. Car park. – Footpaths from Kamp-Bornhofen: an easy walk of 30 minutes. By the steeper mountain path 15 minutes walk. – Open to the public at all times.

Marksburg Castle above Braubach · Text on page 63

Liebenstein Castle which was built at the end of the 13th century, came into the possession of Nassau-Saarbrücken at an early date. The defensive residential tower which is square-shaped, seems to be growing out of the ground like a stump of rock. The seven-storey keep is partially preserved.

Owned by Ludwig Freiherr von Preuschen, Osterspai/Rh. Inhabited. Castle restaurant. – Reached by car from Kamp-Bornhofen (B 42) via Burgenstrasse. Car park. – 30 minutes easy walk from Kamp-Bornhofen. 20 minutes walk taking the rather steep mountain path via Sterrenberg Castle. – Castle ruins open to the public at all times.

The Castle in Boppard

The Elector Balduin of Trier constructed one of the most formidable fortified buildings in the central Rhine area. The castle was built on the banks of the Rhine in order to consolidate the archiepiscopal rule that had been forced on the people of Boppard following the rebellion of 1327. At the end of 1499 the castle was destroyed by a big fire. But only a year later it was already rebuilt. However, the keep escaped damage in the fire. This is proved by the frescoes dating from the 2nd half of the 14th century to be seen on the top floor which made Balduin's castle an important place of interest. The castle houses the municipal local history museum and the District Court.

Owned by town of Boppard. Local history, museum wood and forest museum. – Reached by car from the A 14, B 9 or B 42. Car park. – Open to the public on Mondays, Wednesdays and Sundays from 10 a. m. to 12 noon, on Saturdays from 10. a. m. to 12 noon and from 3 p. m. to 5 p. m. from May to the end of September.

The Marksburg (Marksburg Castle) Pictures on pages 9, 61, 62

This castle towering on a high crag above Braubach, is the only fully preserved medieval fortress on the Rhine. At the beginning of the 13th century it was first known as "Brubach Castle" and belonged to the Lords of Eppstein. In the 13th century it passed into the possession of the Counts of Katzenelnbogen who turned it into a fortress. From 1479 to 1803 the Marksburg, as it was known from the 15th century onwards, was under the uninterrupted rule of the Landgraves of Hesse. In 1866 the castle together with the town of Braubach belonged to Prussia and in 1899 Wilhelm II.

63

The kitchen in Marksburg Castle · Text on page 63

presented it to the "*Association for the Preservation of German Castles*" which had been founded in that same year. This association commissioned Bodo Ebhardt with the task of restoring it on the basis of structural drawings by Wilhelm Dilich (about 1607) and of fitting it out as a typical fortress of the late Middle Ages.

Located round a triangular courtyard are three asymmetrical wings of the building. The South side from which enemy attacks were to be expected, is protected by the "Kaiser Heinrich Tower" like a massive coat of armour. Behind a no less mighty wall is the East wing with the magnificent palas or living quarters together with kitchen, women's apartments and the Knights' Hall on the upper floor. The ancient keep rises from the centre of the courtyard. It is 40 metres high and has a commanding view of the countryside and is naturally also visible from afar. The circular top of the tower which was 8 metres high, was destroyed by the artillery of the 20th century in March 1945. It had previously been restored on the basis of Dilich's plans in 1906. But thanks to considerable state grants after the war, it was possible to repair the severe damage including that suffered by the keep itself so that the castle as a whole could be preserved. An irreplaceable cultural monument, "a superb example of medieval fortified and domestic architecture" (Magnus Backes) is today one of the most notable places of interest in the central Rhine region.

Owned by: Deutsche Burgenvereinigung e. V. Burgenforschungsinstitut. – Museum. Library of the above-named organization. Archives. – Reached by car from Braubach; car park. – 15 minutes walk from the town centre via Sommergasse; along the Rhine via Weinbergspfad, Martinskapelle – 40 minutes walk. – This castle – the only undestroyed hilltop castle on the central Rhine – is open to visitors at all times. Enquire at Castle Administration (Tel. 0 26 27/2 06).

The Martinsburg in Oberlahnstein   Picture on page 69

The Martinsburg with its hexagonal keep was built on the banks of the Rhine at Oberlahnstein at the end of the 14th century and was used by the Electors of Mainz for the levying of tolls. Like the Trier bishops' castle in Boppard and that of the Cologne bishops in Andernach it was originally protected against the town by ramparts and ditches. The buildings are arranged round a square courtyard and display the architectural styles prevailing from the 14th to the 18th centuries. The palas or living quarters was built in 1500

Stolzenfels Castle above Kapellen · Text on page 67

and in 1712 the Gothic building was converted to the Baroque style. Today the Martinsburg houses the offices of local authorities as well as private apartments.

Owned by the Land Rhineland-Palatinate. Used partly by local authorities. – Reached by car from Oberlahnstein. – Not open to the public.

Lahneck Castle
Picture on page 70

Lahneck Castle is situated at the point where the River Lahn flows into the Rhine and is in a dominating position on the hill-top near Oberlahnstein. It was built in about the year 1240 as the most northerly fortress of the Mainz Electors. Around 1460 Dieter von Isenburg had the castle considerably strengthened by the construction of a new outlying protective wall. In the middle of the side exposed to attack to the south is the five-sided keep. On both sides of the keep a massive protective wall three and a half metres thick gives protection to the parts of the castle beyond, especially the palas or living quarters which forms the north wing facing away from the side most open to attack. By 1688 the castle had fallen into complete ruin but in 1860 it was restored to its original state.

Owned by Erbengemeinschaft Mischke Dr. Frhr. v. Preuschen. Inhabited, restaurant open throughout the year with garden terrace and café. – Reached by car from the B 42. Car park. – 15 minutes walk from bus stop. Along motorway 30 minutes. – Open to the public daily from Easter to October, courtyard, chapel, Knights' Hall, ascent of the tower. Open-air theatre August and September.

Stolzenfels Castle
Pictures on pages 65, 66

Stolzenfels Castle is situated half-way up the hillside opposite the mouth of the River Lahn, a few kilometres above Koblenz. This former toll fortress belonging to the Electors of Trier, was started by Archbishop Arnold II. about the year 1250 and the electoral princes liked living there. But since the French invasion of 1689 it had been in ruins. The city of Koblenz made a gift of the ruins to Friedrich Wilhelm IV., later King of Prussia. Between 1825 and 1842 he had it rebuilt at considerable expense on the basis of plans by the most famous architect of his time, Karl Friedrich *Schinkel*. Although in restoring the castle the medieval sections were preserved, "a princely residence was

Bed-chamber in Stolzenfels Castle · Text on page 67

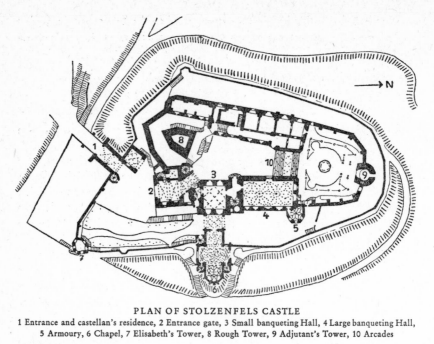

PLAN OF STOLZENFELS CASTLE
1 Entrance and castellan's residence, 2 Entrance gate, 3 Small banqueting Hall, 4 Large banqueting Hall,
5 Armoury, 6 Chapel, 7 Elisabeth's Tower, 8 Rough Tower, 9 Adjutant's Tower, 10 Arcades

created on the wooded heights in the neo-Gothic style and influenced some-
what by English castle architecture. However, it faithfully reflected the spirit
of the age and of the royal master's wishes" (Paul Clemen). On the outside
wall two murals by Lasinsky portray historical episodes. The furnishings of
the living rooms date from the first half of the 19th century. In 1853 Ernst
Deger adorned the Castle Chapel walls with paintings which are among the
most mature works of the Düsseldorf Nazarene school. Today the castle is a
museum. From the terrace one has a view of the village of Kapellen at the
foot of the mountain, overlooking the mouth of the River Lahn, Oberlahnstein and Niederlahnstein and downstream as far as Koblenz and Ehrenbreitstein.

Owned by the Land Rhineland-Palatinate. Museum. – Not directly accessible by car.
Car park below the castle. – 10 minutes walk from Kapellen. – Open to the public
with conducted tours throughout the year. For special guided tours apply to the
Castle Administration, Kapellen-Stolzenfels (Telephone: Koblenz 9 06/3 26 56).

Martinsburg Castle in Oberlahnstein · Text on page 64

Ehrenbreitstein

Picture on page 73

The dominant hill facing Koblenz at the junction of the Rhine and the Moselle, is not only an outstanding feature of the landscape but was for centuries a point of the utmost strategic importance. Here the largest and most formidable Rhine fortress next to the Rheinfels at St. Goar, had been built. The Archbishops of Trier had the fortress constructed in the second half of the 12th century and at the end of the 14th century. In the years that followed practically every generation worked on it until ultimately it became the massive Renaissance fortress as depicted by Merian's engraving of 1646. In 1801 it was demolished by the French. But after the annexation of the Rhineland, it was rebuilt in the years 1815–32 by Prussia under the supervision of Colonel von Aster and became one of the biggest fortresses in Europe. And so it has remained although today it serves only peaceful purposes. Ehrenbreitstein houses: *the State Museum of History and Folklore (Land Museum of Technical Antiquities) and Rhine Museum* as well as a Youth Hostel.

Owned by the Land Rhineland-Palatinate. 2 restaurants. Youth Hostel. Film archives. Two museums (the Rhine Museum is the oldest river museum in the world). Open daily from 10 a. m. to 6 p. m. except Fridays. Fortress installations. – Reached by car from Ehrenbreitstein or via Niederberg. Car park by the fortress. – Chairlift. – 20 minutes walk from the B 42.

The Archbishop's Castle in Andernach

Picture on page 74

The castle in Andernach is the most magnificent of all Rhine town castles. Like the castle built in Boppard by the Elector Balduin, it was constructed by the Cologne Electors as a citadel, being protected against the town by a moat. In 1355 the townsfolk of Boppard stormed the castle and burnt it down. In 1491 it was rebuilt by Hermann von Hesse. In 1689 the French laid it in ruins again. All that remained were the rounded corner tower made of basalt lava from the Eifel Hills, three storeys high and above it the guard house with the protruding walled passage whence one has a fine view of the surrounding countryside, and the outer walls of the palas or living quarters.

Owned by the Land Rhineland-Palatinate. Youth Hostel. – Reached by car from Andernach. Car park at Stadtgraben. – Open to the public at all times as the ruins are situated in a public park.

71

Lahneck Castle above Oberlahnstein · Text on page 67

Hammerstein Castle

Picture on page 77

The formidable rock with the ruins of this once so mighty castle dominate an extensive stretch of the Rhine valley. The castle was first mentioned as early as the year 1002 as the seat of the Hammerstein family. In 1020 it was conquered by Heinrich II. and made an imperial castle. Having been considerably enlarged by the Emperor Heinrich IV., it was used by him as a refuge when he was pursued by his son Heinrich V. and he brought with him the entire crown insignia. In 1374 it passed into the tenure of the Electors of Trier. It was only after the Thirty Years' War that this castle, which Merian's engraving portrays in its full medieval splendour, was razed and destroyed. Today all that remains of the vast structure are ruins apart from the massive keep and the outer wall which has the tremendous thickness of 5 metres.

Owned by the family of the Barons of Hammerstein.

Rheineck Castle

This castle which was built by the Counts of the Palatinate on a wooded hill-top between Brohl and Bad Niederbreisig, was besieged and destroyed by the German King Konrad III. in 1151. In 1164 Rainald von Dassel, Archbishop of Cologne took possession of it. In 1282 Rheineck was destroyed for the second time. On this occasion Rudolf von Habsburg was responsible. Afterwards the Cologne Electors had the castle rebuilt and then in 1689 it shared the fate of most other Rhine castles. In 1832 an entirely new building was erected there by Joseph Carl von *Lassaulx*. All that remained of the original castle were the 20 metre high keep built of square blocks of stone and the Romanesque chapel. The paintings were done by Eduard von Steinle on behalf of the owner, Moritz August von Bethmann-Hollweg, for many years curator of Bonn University.

Owned by Seilbahn GmbH., Altenahr. Partly inhabited. Museum. Restaurant. – Reached by car from the lower terminal of the funicular railway. – Funicular (chairlift). – 30 minutes walk from the lower funicular station. – Open to the public from April to October (Enquiries: Telephone Brohl 0 26 33/7 12).

The Fortress of Ehrenbreitstein · Text on page 71

Arenfels Castle

Arenfels near Bad Hönningen, is one of the castles that came off worst through conversion into the neo-Gothic style. This castle with its early Gothic keep was founded by the Counts of Isenburg around 1260. The two circular towers on the North front were added during the late Gothic period, whilst the 16th and 17th centuries brought the addition of the most beautiful Renaissance and Baroque parts. This "wonderfully stirring group of buildings" underwent changes at the hands of the Cologne Cathedral architect Zwirner in the middle of last century whose "rigid unit construction style failed to do it justice" (Paul Clemen).

Owned by Baroness von Geyr. Inhabited. Restaurant. – Reached by car from Bad Hönningen. Car park. – 15 minutes walk from Bad Hönningen. – Not open to the public.

Landskron Castle

The Staufen fortress of Landskron is situated in the Ahr Valley near Bad Neuenahr on a cone-shaped hill and it dominates the surrounding countryside. It was built by King Philipp of Swabia at the beginning of the 13th century not far from the point where the River Ahr flows into the Rhine. It was intended as a citadel against the Electors of Cologne and as a protection for the ancient Coronation Route from Aachen to Frankfurt. The ruins still testify to the former greatness of the castle which was destroyed in the 17th century, later passed into the possession of the Imperial Baron vom Stein and which today still belongs to his descendants.

Owned by Graf von Canitz, Nassau/Lahn. – Reached by car via Lohrsdorf (bad road surface). Car park. – 25 minutes walk from Heimersheim, 30 minutes from Heppingen and 45 minutes from Lohrsdorf. – Open ruins on view at all times.

Dattenberg Castle

The castle which was a tenure of the Cologne Electors, was occupied by the Lords of Dadenberg, first mention of whom was in the 13th century. All

75

The Archbishop's Castle in Andernach · Text on page 71

that remains of the medieval castle are the Romanesque tower, the keep and the moat. The former palace has been converted into a youth training centre.

Owned by Landkreis Cologne. Youth Hostel. – Reached by car from Linz station. – 20 minutes walk from Linz. – Not open to the public.

The Castle in Linz

The Cologne electoral castle situated on the Rhine front was built by Archbishop Engelbert in 1368. All that remains of it today is the tower crowned with a late Gothic superstructure in 1599. Everything else was changed in the Baroque period.

Owned by the town of Linz. Inhabited. – Reached by car. – Not open to the public.

Ockenfels Castle

Ockenfels Castle near Linz was the ancestral home of the zur Leyen family who had acquired it on tenure from the Cologne Electors. It was destroyed in 1475. The Cologne architect Rheinhardt rebuilt it from the ruins.

Owned by Hermann May. Hotel, Restaurant. – Reached by car from Linz. Car park. – 30 minutes walk from Linz. – Open to the public at all times.

Roland's Arch   **Picture on page 78**

The ivy-clad, legendary ashlar window that once looked down on to the Rhine island of Nonnenwerth, represents the last remains of Rolandseck Castle which was built in about the year 1100 by the Cologne Archbishop Friedrich. In 1334 it was refortified and then, in the fighting between the Cologne Electors and Emperor Friedrich III in the 15th century, it was destroyed. When the arch collapsed in the stormy night of New Year's Eve 1840, the poet Ferdinand Freiligrath, then living in Unkel, published an appeal in the "Kölnische Zeitung" for funds with which to rebuild the arch:

The ruins of Hammerstein · Text on page 72

"It is up to you! I stand here with begging hands,
Up and down the Rhine I walk, admonishing as I go.
Attendant of Roland, I hasten through the country;
Open helmet in outstretched hand,
I appeal to you: restore his arch to him."

The many donations received from castle-lovers all over the world enabled the arch to be rebuilt, the work being carried out by the Cologne Cathedral architect Ernst Zwirner. The owner of the Roland's Arch, Princess Marianne of Prussia, was at first angered by the autocratic action of the self-styled "Roland's attendant" Freiligrath. But ultimately she gave her consent and herself made a generous contribution to the cost of building a new elementary school in Rolandswerth.

Owned by Grand-Duke Ernst-Ludwig of Hesse and Rhine, Darmstadt. Restaurant. – Reached by car from Mehlem to Rodderberg. – From here 15 minutes walk. From Rolandseck 30 minutes walk. – Open ruins always on view.

Drachenfels Castle

Picture on page 81

The wild, jagged Drachenfels towering so mightily above the river is not the only one of the Seven Mountains to have had a castle at its top. Other peaks of the "Septimontium", as these wooded hills were called as long ago as the 8th century, were crowned with castles, such as the *Wolkenburg* and the *Löwenburg*. But only very scanty ruins of these castles are left. Visible far and wide, however, is the rugged keep of the Drachenfels built for the Cologne Electors, which is one of the rarer examples of a true ashlar structure. The view from the hill-top which is 321 metres high, is probably the most famous on the Rhine, just as the ruins themselves have rightly been described by Edmund Renard as "the proudest and most popular of the entire valley of the Rhine". On clear days the volcanic mountains of the Eifel can be seen, from the Laacher See to the "Hohe Acht". And to the north the spires of Cologne Cathedral can be seen.

This formidable mountain castle was started by the Cologne Archbishop Arnold I. (1138–1151). In 1149 it passed in tenure to the Bonn Cassius Foundation, whose dean, Gerhard von Are completed it by the year 1167.

79

Roland's Arch with view of the Drachenfels beyond · Text on page 76

In 1176 the Cassius Foundation appointed the Knight Godart as the castle bailiff and his family adopted the name of the mountain and used the silver dragon facing to the right on a red background at its coat of arms. The legend of Siegfried is linked with this symbol for it was he who is said to have slain the dragon living in the mountain cave and to have bathed in its blood. Today the word "dragon's blood" has a more agreeable meaning, for it is the name given to the red wine produced from the vines growing on the southwest slopes of the mountain.

During the turmoil in and around Cologne from 1582 to 1586, the castle was vainly besieged. During the Thirty Years' War the castle was occupied in turn by the Swedes and the Spaniards to the pain and anguish of the people living in its vicinity. The Elector, therefore, ordered the castle to be demolished in 1634 and this was done with great thoroughness so that by 1642 one only spoke of the Drachenfels "ruins".

When work started on the building of Cologne Cathedral in the 13th century, the Drachenfels had to surrender its valuable trachyte stones. In fact the spot where the stone quarries lay is today still known locally as the "Cathedral hole". Finally, continued irresponsible mining caused the castle to collapse. In 1780 the Castle Chapel collapsed and in the autumn of 1813, the last of the Burgraves, Max Friedrich von Gudenau had to leave his residence there. In 1820 the outer works of the castle plunged to the depths. And when even the top of the mountain itself was to be cut away, the Prussian government intervened, gained possession of the mountain-top and protected the ruins from further decay.

Owned by the Land North Rhine Westphalia, – Castle restaurant. – Reached by car from Königswinter but only via Weingartenweg as far as Lemmerzbad Swimming Pool. Car park. – From here, 30 minutes walk; from Königswinter via Eselsweg (donkey path) 45 minutes; via Nachtigallental 50 minutes; and from Rhöndorf 45 minutes. – Electric cog railway from Königswinter. – Open to the public all the year round – open ruins.

Godesburg Castle

Picture on page 82

Even in Roman times the basalt hill rising from the plain had a Shrine on the top. The name Godesberg is derived from Wotanberg from which it can be deduced that it had once been a Germanic place of sacrifice. The Wotan cult changed in the course of the Christian era to that of St. Michael.

The ruins of Drachenfels Castle above Königswinter · Text on page 79

The *Chapel,* whose place has since been taken by the delightful Baroque building of 1697 (the stucco decoration was the work of Giovanni Pietro Castelli) was already there in the early Romanesque period, as pointed out by Paul Clemen.

The medieval castle was founded by Archbishop Theoderich of Cologne in 1210. The great Archbishop Konrad von Are-Hochstaden added the massive, 10 metre thick tower in about the middle of the 13th century. In 1343 Walram von Jülich added to it, making it half as high again (32 metres) and fortified the entire length of the castle.

The Godesburg is one of the greatest military fortresses in the northern part of the Rhineland and, for a long time, it was the favourite residence of the archbishops of Cologne. In the Cologne War against the Cologne Archbishop Gebhard Truchsess von Waldburg, who had become a convert to Protestantism, it was demolished by the troops of Archbishop Ernst of Bavaria. After being rebuilt once again, it was finally destroyed by the French in 1794.

Owned by the town of Bad Godesberg. Restaurant and hotel. – Reached by car from Bad Godesberg via Burgstrasse/Winterstrasse. Car park. – 15 minutes walk from Aennchenstrasse and Burgstrasse. – Open to the public with ascent of the tower at all times.

Godesburg Castle · Text on page 80

"THE RHINELANDS" COLLECTION

Selected studies on the history, art and lore
of the Rhinelands

The following have so far appeared:

BURGEN IM MOSELTAL

LAND AN DER AHR

RÖMER AM RHEIN

ROMANTISCHER RHEIN

DAS SIEBENGEBIRGE

BAD BERTRICH

MAARE UND VULKANE DER EIFEL

RHEINISCHES WEINLAND

DER ALTE FRIEDHOF IN BONN

BUNDESHAUPTSTADT BONN

To appear soon:

ROMANTIK AM RHEIN

RHEINISCHE MADONNEN

WILHELM STOLLFUSS VERLAG BONN